Natural State Notables

Notables

Steven Teske

Natural State Notables
21 Famous People from Arkansas

Steven Teske

Butler Center Books
Little Rock, Arkansas

The Butler Center for Arkansas Studies
Central Arkansas Library System
100 Rock Street
Little Rock, AR 72201

First printing: February 2013

ISBN (13) 978-1-935106-52-4
ISBN (10) 1-935106-52-x

Project director: Rod Lorenzen
Copyeditor/proofreader: Ali Welky
Book design: Michael Keckhaver

Library of Congress Cataloging-in-Publication Data

Teske, Steven, 1962-
  Natural state notables: 21 famous people from Arkansas/Steven Teske.
    pages cm
  ISBN-13: 978-1-935106-52-4 (paperback : alkaline paper)
  ISBN-10: 1-935106-52-X (paperback : alkaline paper)
  1. Arkansas—Biography—Juvenile literature. I. Title.
  CT224.T47 2013
  920.0767—dc23

                                             2012027610

This book is printed on archival-quality paper that meets requirements of the American National Standard for Information Sciences, Permanence of Paper, Printed Library Materials, ANSI Z39.48-1984.

This project is supported in part by a grant from the Arkansas Humanities Council and the Department of Arkansas Heritage.

The publishing division of the Butler Center for Arkansas Studies was made possible by the generosity of Dora Johnson Ragsdale & John G. Ragsdale Jr.

Printed in Canada

TABLE OF CONTENTS

ACKNOWLEDGEMENTS

None of the notable people in this book became famous by working alone. Whether they are famous for writing, for music, for athletics, for politics, or for business, they had the help and support of many other people. In the same way, this book would not have been possible without the help of many people. Just finding the pictures and getting permission to use them involved dozens of people, too many to name.

Among those I would especially like to thank—because without them, *Natural State Notables* never would have been written—are Dr. Bobby Roberts of the Central Arkansas Library System (CALS), who first suggested the idea for this book; Dr. Kay Bland of CALS's Butler Center for Arkansas Studies, who has provided much support and inspiration along the way; Rod Lorenzen, director of Butler Center Books, who guided this book through the publishing process; Ali Welky, the copyeditor who checked every sentence and made many improvements; and Michael Keckhaver, the designer who put it all together and made it a book worth reading. I also want to thank my wife and children for their patience and support—especially my youngest daughter, Olivia, who read each chapter of the book and suggested many helpful additions.

PREFACE

What does it mean to be famous? People who are famous have done something that many other people notice. People who write books or play music sometimes become famous. People who play basketball or baseball or football sometimes become famous. People who work in the government or who start a new company sometimes become famous. Many people who do these things are not famous. But when a lot of people notice what they do, they are famous.

This book tells about twenty-one people from Arkansas who are famous. Bill Clinton was elected president of the United States. Sam Walton started the chain of stores called Walmart. Johnny Cash was a musician. A lot of people noticed what Clinton and Walton and Cash were doing. You might already know some things about some of the people in this book. Other people might be new to you.

Not all of these people were born in Arkansas. A few came to Arkansas after they grew up, but the things they did in Arkansas made them famous. Not all these people became famous for things they did in Arkansas. Some were born in the Natural State but went elsewhere before they did the things that made them famous. All twenty-one are Arkansans. And all twenty-one lived and became famous in the last eighty years. Some of them are still alive today.

Many different kinds of people are famous. And people are famous for many different reasons. These twenty-one lives will tell you about Arkansas and its history. These people might also give you ideas about things you can do that other people will notice. Maybe one day you will be another famous person from Arkansas!

Courtesy of the William J. Clinton Presidential Library

Maya Angelou speaks at the Clinton Presidential Center in Little Rock; 2008.

MAYA ANGELOU

is a famous writer and poet. She was born in St. Louis, Missouri, and named Marguerite Annie Johnson. Maya is a nickname for Marguerite that she has used for all of her writing and public appearances. She grew up in Stamps, Arkansas, where her grandmother owned the grocery store. She describes in her books how angry and unhappy she was when she saw that people did not treat each other fairly. Her own family was mocked just because of the color of their skin. She also describes how she did not talk for four years after a man hurt her. A teacher helped her by showing her books written by great writers, including William Shakespeare, Edgar Allan Poe, Paul Laurence Dunbar, and Frederick Douglass. After she graduated from high school, she left Arkansas to live in California. But Angelou never forgot the things that she had learned growing up in Stamps.

Angelou is most famous for the poems and books she has written. She has also been a singer, an actress, and a teacher. She is famous as a political activist, which means that she tries to change things in the world by encouraging leaders and voters to work for the right things. Among the things she considers right are human rights, justice, and peace. She is against racism and hatred. In her books and poems and speeches, she encourages people to find simple solutions for the world's problems. Angelou fills her poems and stories with images of survival, hope, and joy.

Timeline

Born: April 4, 1928

Published *I Know Why the Caged Bird Sings*: 1970

"I have found that among its other benefits, giving liberates the soul of the giver."

Her most famous book, *I Know Why the Caged Bird Sings*, describes her childhood in Arkansas. She has lived in Africa, both in Egypt and Ghana, as well as in several parts of the United States. In 1993, she read a new poem, "On the Pulse of Morning," at the inauguration of President Bill Clinton. A movie made that same year, *Poetic Justice*, features poems written by Angelou being read by singer Janet Jackson.

Angelou has won countless awards for her writing and for her political activism. Her books are still used in schools in Arkansas and around the world. Those books inspire students to work for justice and peace.

Stamps

Courtesy of the Arkansas Democrat-Gazette, copyright 2012

Maya Angelou reading "On the Pulse of Morning" at Bill Clinton's inauguration; 1993.

Thanksgiving dinner, November 1957, with L. C. and Daisy Bates and Little Rock Nine students.

DAISY BATES

is best remembered as a political activist. She worked to change the laws of Arkansas so that all people would have equal rights. She was born in Huttig, Arkansas, where she was raised by foster parents, Orlee and Susan Smith. She attended a segregated school. This means that all the students in her school were African American. So were all the teachers. Another segregated school in Huttig had only white students and white teachers. Throughout the state of Arkansas, all the schools were segregated. When she was fifteen years old, she met L. C. Bates, a traveling salesman. They were married in 1942. Even before their marriage, they worked together in Little Rock, Arkansas. They ran a

newspaper for African Americans called the *Arkansas State Press*.

In 1954, the Supreme Court of the United States ruled that schools should be desegregated. This means that African American students and white students would attend the same schools. Some cities in Arkansas—such as Charleston, Fayetteville, and Hoxie—quickly combined their school systems. Other cities, including Little Rock, were much slower to desegregate their schools. Bates and her husband believed that desegregation should happen quickly. In a court case in 1956, she testified about the need to allow all the students in Little Rock to attend any school. Bates also insisted that she be treated with the same amount of respect that was given to white witnesses. The next year, nine

Timeline

Born: circa 1913

Worked with Little Rock Nine: 1957–58

> *"We will walk until we are free, until we can walk to any school and take our children to any school in the United States."*

African American students enrolled at Little Rock Central High School. Daisy and L. C. Bates supported and encouraged those nine students. Though the students were insulted and threatened, they were able to attend classes. One of them graduated the following May. Throughout their ordeal, Bates and other people supported and encouraged the nine students. They reminded them that their success would help to change the laws in Arkansas and would make life better for many other people. Bates also spoke publicly on behalf of the group. She helped national organizations, including the National Association for the Advancement of Colored People (NAACP), to remain in contact with the students and their other supporters.

Bates moved to New York in 1960. She was on the board of the NAACP until 1970. In 1963, she spoke to the same crowd in Washington DC that heard Dr. Martin Luther King Jr.'s famous "I Have a Dream" speech. She returned to Arkansas in 1968, living in Mitchellville and working to overcome poverty. Several Arkansas cities have named streets for her. The third Monday in February each year is a state holiday in Arkansas dedicated to her memory.

Courtesy of Special Collections, University of Arkansas Libraries, Fayetteville

Daisy Bates; circa 1960.

RUTH BEALL (1896–1974)

Courtesy of Arkansas Children's Hospital

Ruth Beall; 1961.

NOT MANY PEOPLE

recognize the name of Ruth Beall. The result of her work, though, is world famous. Beall saved Arkansas Children's Hospital in Little Rock from closing during the Great Depression. For almost thirty years, she was superintendent of the hospital. With Beall in charge, the hospital grew and was able to help more children than ever before.

Beall was born in Missouri and grew up there, but her family moved to Rogers, Arkansas, when she was a college student. During World War I, she worked with the American Red Cross in Rogers. After the war was over, Beall worked for an organization that was trying to help people overcome a dangerous sickness called tuberculosis. Beall also visited schools, handing out free toothbrushes and toothpaste to poor children and teaching them how to brush their teeth. In 1934, she brought a boy from Rogers to the hospital in Little Rock because he was sick with tuberculosis. She complained to the director of the hospital that the building was run-down. She also pointed out that not enough people were working there to take care of the children. The director asked her if she would take the job as superintendent of the hospital. If she did, she could try to fix the problems that she saw. Beall agreed to take the job. Her first task was to find enough money to keep

Timeline

Born: 1896   Became superintendent of Arkansas Children's Hospital: February 1, 1934

"How are we going to continue to serve our children in the future as we have in the past?"

---

the hospital open. In one month, she was able to raise thirty thousand dollars. She used all of that money to help the hospital.

For the next twenty-seven years, Beall continued to help children by keeping the hospital open and by improving it in every way she could. Beall ate a simple diet of cheese sandwiches to save money so more could be spent helping sick children. She treated each patient at the hospital as if he or she was her own child. Sometimes this meant fighting with doctors and other adults to make sure that the children were treated well. Once she made a doctor miss giving a speech to other doctors, telling him, "Anybody can make that speech. Only you can save this child." Rather than sitting in her office, she was often found walking up and down the halls of the hospital, making sure that things were being done in the right way. One magazine writer called her "The Terrible-Tempered Angel of Arkansas." When she retired in 1961, the hospital

directors gave her a retirement salary that included money for the payments on her home. They also bought her a new car. "It was a very challenging job and I loved it," Beall said, "but the only thing I will miss is my patients."

Rogers

Little Rock

Ruth Beall with children and an elephant friend; 1954.

Courtesy of Arkansas Children's Hospital

Johnny Cash with his wife, June Carter Cash; 1983.

JOHNNY CASH

was born in Kingsland, Arkansas. Three years later, his family moved to Dyess. Dyess was a colony in Arkansas for people who wanted to farm but had lost all their money in the Great Depression. Cash learned how to sing and play the guitar while he lived in Dyess. After serving in the United States Army, Cash was married in Texas and returned to the area where he had grown up, living in Memphis, Tennessee. With two friends, Cash formed a band and played at Sun Records in Memphis, where they made their first record. Like other musicians for Sun Records (including Elvis Presley),

Cash and his friends performed in concerts in the small towns around Memphis, including many towns and cities in eastern Arkansas.

Cash's music became very popular. He sold millions of records with songs such as "I Walk the Line," "Ring of Fire," and, "A Boy Named Sue." He acted in four movies and also appeared on many TV shows, including two that were named for him. Both were called *The Johnny Cash Show*. One was shown every week from 1969 until 1971, and the other was shown during the summer of 1976. Cash was famous for singing songs about people who were poor, unlucky, or in trouble. One of his most famous concerts

Timeline

Born: February 26, 1932   First recordings: 1955

> *"My work life has been simple: cotton as a youth and music as an adult."*

was performed in a prison in California. Cash became known as the Man in Black because of the black clothes he usually wore in concerts and on TV. In 1968, Cash divorced his first wife and married fellow musician June Carter.

Johnny Cash never forgot the state where he had grown up and learned about music. He often performed concerts in Arkansas, not only in large cities like Little Rock and Fayetteville but also in Fordyce, near where he had been born, and in Dyess, where he had grown up. During his long career, he remained very popular in Arkansas and throughout the United States. His music is still heard today.

Johnny Cash at Cummins Prison talking with inmates; 1969.

First number-one songs: 1958   Died: September 12, 2003

Courtesy of the William J. Clinton Presidential Library

Presidential portrait of Bill Clinton, 1999.

BILL CLINTON

was the forty-second president of the United States. He is the only president to come from Arkansas. Clinton was born in Hope, Arkansas, and grew up in Hot Springs. His family was not rich. He learned from family members and from neighbors how to work hard to make life better. After finishing high school, Clinton attended colleges outside of Arkansas. He returned in 1973 with a degree in law and taught classes at the University of Arkansas in Fayetteville. He ran for Congress in 1974 but lost. He married Hillary Rodham in 1975. He ran for attorney general of Arkansas in 1976 and won. He ran for governor of Arkansas six times and won five elections, serving as governor from 1979 to 1981 and from 1983 to 1992. His Presidential Library is in Little Rock, and he often returns to his home state.

While he was governor, Clinton worked hard to make Arkansas a better place for people to live. He wanted teachers to be paid more money and to be better prepared to teach. He wanted better roads so people could travel more easily, and so food and other supplies could be brought into Arkansas's cities and towns. He wanted to encourage new businesses to build in Arkansas so people would have more jobs. Some people were angry at Governor Clinton. They said he was making them pay too much money in taxes for all these improvements. One reason Clinton lost the election in 1980 was that people were unhappy about taxes. Clinton won his other elections, though, because a lot of people in Arkansas agreed with him about the things Arkansas needed.

Timeline

Born: August 19, 1946

Ran for Congress: 1974

"There is nothing wrong with America that cannot be cured by what is right with America."

When he ran for president, Clinton said, "I still believe in a place called Hope." He wanted the same things for the country that he had wanted for Arkansas, including better schools and more jobs. While he was president, he worked with Congress to make sure that the country did not spend more money than it received through taxes. He also tried to make sure that the money spent by the United States government helped people. Sometimes he and the Congress disagreed about what was best for the country. Fights about politics were often bigger news than the things the president and Congress were trying to do. Bill Clinton was very proud to be able to say that the United States gained 22 million new jobs during the eight years he was president. He also worked hard to help people in other countries. He helped protect people from harmful governments in places like Haiti and Bosnia. He also worked to stop the fighting in places like Ireland and the Middle East. Since the end of his presidency in 2001, Bill Clinton has continued trying to make life better for people in the United States and around the world. He has never forgotten the lessons about people he learned growing up in Arkansas.

Courtesy of the Butler Center for Arkansas Studies, Central Arkansas Library System

Bill Clinton running for Congress; 1974.

Governor of Arkansas: 1979–1981, 1983–1992   President of the United States: 1993–2001

William Dillard; circa 1980s.

WILLIAM DILLARD

created the chain of stores called Dillard's. These stores sell clothing for men, women, and children. They also sell home furnishings, such as sofas, beds, and dining room sets. Dillard opened his first store in Nashville, Arkansas, in 1938. There are now 330 Dillard's stores in 29 states in the country.

Dillard was born in Mineral Springs, Arkansas, not far from Nashville, in 1914. His father, Thomas Dillard, was a farmer who also ran a store in Mineral Springs.

Dillard worked in his father's store while he was growing up and knew that he wanted to spend his life in that business. He went to college at the University of Arkansas in Fayetteville, earning a degree in accounting. He then went to a college in New York, earning a master's degree in business. The next year, he opened his Nashville store, using the same name as his father's store, T. J. Dillard's. He married Alexa Latimer in 1940. In 1948, Dillard sold his store in Nashville and opened a new store in Texarkana. He then opened another store in Magnolia in 1955, beginning the Dillard's chain of stores. At that time, Dillard liked to buy stores that were struggling to stay open. Rather than paying to put up new buildings, he would remodel the building to fit what he wanted to sell. Over the next few years, he added stores in Texas and Oklahoma to his growing chain of Arkansas stores.

In 1963, Dillard moved to Little

Timeline

Born: September 2, 1914   Opened first store: February 12, 1938   Established Little Rock as

"Business without integrity is not good business—and in the long run will not be successful."

Rock, Arkansas. He bought two downtown buildings that had been other stores, called Pfeifer's and Blass. In 1965, he opened a Dillard's store in Little Rock's Park Plaza Mall. Dillard realized that many Americans preferred to shop in malls rather than in downtown stores. As his chain continued to grow, Dillard's stores opened in shopping malls in many cities. The company usually opened a new store with attention-grabbing ceremonies. They worked closely with local newspapers to promote their stores and draw in business. Dillard's also stayed ahead of its competition by using computers to keep track of the company's buying and selling. Other chains of stores began to imitate Dillard's in its use of computers and in its development of the suburban shopping mall. In 1999, Dillard was one of the first four business leaders to be inducted into the Arkansas Business Hall of Fame.

William Dillard as a young man.

---

homebase for Dillard's: 1964   Opened first Dillard's mall stores: 1965   Died: February 8, 2002

Photo by Ernie Deane; Courtesy of the Arkansas History Commission

Jimmy Driftwood; circa 1964.

JIMMY DRIFTWOOD

was a schoolteacher, a singer, and a songwriter. The most famous of his six thousand songs is "The Battle of New Orleans," which was a number-one hit in the United States in 1959. Driftwood's real name was James Corbitt Morris. He was born in West Richwoods, which is in Stone County, Arkansas. He began teaching school when he was sixteen years old, even before he had finished high school. Continuing to take classes, Driftwood taught in several small country schools in northern Arkansas. He finished high school in 1928 and took college classes from Arkansas State Teachers College in Conway and from John Brown College in Siloam Springs.

He married Cleda Johnson in 1936. He did not finish college until 1949. Even so, he continued to be a successful teacher for the rest of his life. He wrote "The Battle of New Orleans" in 1936 to help his students understand the War of 1812.

Driftwood loved to play the fiddle and also the guitar. He especially loved the folk songs of the Ozark Mountains. In the 1950s, he began submitting songs and recordings to music companies. At first they were not interested. When Chet Atkins helped Driftwood record an album in 1958, some people paid attention to his music. The next year, Johnny Horton recorded one of Driftwood's songs from that album, "The Battle of New Orleans." The song became a number-one hit in the United States, remaining at the top of the country music charts for ten weeks and at the top of the popular music charts for six weeks. The song won Song of the Year at the next Grammy Awards, and several other songs by Driftwood also were nominated for awards.

Driftwood and his wife owned a 150-acre farm in Stone County.

Timeline

Born: June 20, 1907

Composed "The Battle of New Orleans": 1936

"Everything I ever was, everything I am, is back here [in Arkansas]."

From that property, they worked to preserve and promote the native music of the Ozark region. With their friends, they began the Rackensack Folklore Society and started the Arkansas Folk Festival in Mountain View. They also began to organize the Ozark Folk Center. Driftwood used his influence in the state and around the country to raise money for the folk center. He also used that influence to persuade the national government to preserve the Buffalo River and Blanchard Springs Caverns. Although Driftwood died in 1998, his recordings are still played around the world, especially in northern Arkansas. The Ozark culture he worked to preserve attracts thousands of tourists yearly to Arkansas from around the world.

Siloam Springs

Mtn. View

West Richwoods

Conway

Jimmy Driftwood; circa 1955.

Photo by Ernie Deane, Courtesy of the Arkansas History Commission

Al Green recording at the Royal Studios in Memphis.

WHEN HE WAS BORN in Forrest City, Arkansas, in 1946, his name was Albert Greene. When he became famous as a singer, he shortened both his first and last names and has been known ever since as Al Green. Green has sung various kinds of music throughout his career—pop, rock, soul, gospel, and rhythm & blues. He is the pastor of a church in Memphis, Tennessee, and Green continues to sing in concerts all over the world and to record new music.

Green's parents, Robert and Cora Greene, had ten children. The twelve Greenes lived in a two-room house near Forrest City. Robert was a sharecropper, which means that he worked on a farm owned by another person and had to share earnings from the farm with its owner. Green and his brothers sang gospel music in many of the churches around Forrest City. When Green was nine, his family moved to Michigan, where his father found a better-paying job. The family continued to sing gospel music in churches. Green's father kicked him out of the group when he caught him listening to popular rock music.

In Michigan, Green joined with other musicians to form a singing group that they called Al Green and the Soul Mates. A musician from Tennessee heard Green and his group's music and persuaded Green to move to Memphis and record for his company. Green's music became very successful. In the early 1970s, he had seven songs reach the Top Ten list in popular rock music in-

Timeline

Born: April 13, 1946   First (and only) number-one song: 1971

cluding the number-one hit "Let's Stay Together." Those successes were followed by sad times. In 1974, a friend of Green's attacked him in his home, burned him with hot food, and then shot herself. In 1979, Green fell off a stage while performing in Ohio. Green decided that he was not meant to be singing popular music. Using money from his singing career, he bought a church in Memphis, not far from Elvis Presley's mansion, Graceland. Green became the pastor of that church. He also added a recording studio to its property, where he recorded himself and other musicians singing gospel music.

Green's music has always been very popular in Arkansas, as it is all over the world. In 1996, Green was one of the first people inducted into the Arkansas Entertainers Hall of Fame in Pine Bluff. Since 2000, Green has returned to singing his popular music from the early 1970s, as well as gospel music and soul music. As a pastor in Memphis, he is frequently asked to conduct weddings for fans of his music. Those fans travel from as far away as Japan to be married by Green.

Forrest City

Al Green at the Peabody Hotel in Memphis

Photo courtesy of Clay Patrick McBride

Courtesy of Greene & Sandell

Bette Greene in her home; 2012.

BETTE GREENE

grew up in Parkin, Arkansas. Parkin was also the setting for her most famous book, *Summer of My German Soldier*. Her parents, Arthur and Sadie Evensky, owned and operated a dry goods store in Parkin. (A dry goods store sold clothing and other items for the home, but did not sell groceries or hardware. Since the creation of large stores such as Walmart, dry goods stores have become rare.) The Evenskys were the only Jewish family in Parkin.

They attended religious services in Memphis, Tennessee, which is thirty-five miles from Parkin.

After graduating from Central High School in Memphis, she attended several colleges, mostly to participate in writing programs. She married Donald Greene in 1959. She says that her first professional writing assignment happened when she was nine years old. She wrote a story about a barn fire in Parkin. The story was published in the *Commercial Appeal*, a Memphis newspaper. She was paid eighteen cents

Timeline

Born: June 28, 1934 ♦ First paid for writing: 1943 ♦ Novel *Summer of My German Soldier*

for the story. She later worked as a full-time reporter for the same newspaper. She has written seven books as well as many short stories and magazine articles.

Greene's first book was based on her memories of growing up in Parkin. The United States was fighting against Germany, Italy, and Japan in World War II. The United States entered the war in 1941 when Greene was nine years old. Some soldiers captured in Europe from the German and Italian armies were held in prison camps in Arkansas until the war was over. Greene imagined what it might be like if one of those prisoners escaped and if she helped hide him. Those imaginings led to *Summer of My German Solider*. That book was published in 1973 and won several awards, including the *New York Times* Outstanding Book Award. In 1978, a movie was made for television based on her book. *Summer of My German Soldier* starred Kristy McNichol as Patty Bergen, the character in the story who is based on Greene as a girl growing up in Arkansas.

Parkin ●

Courtesy of Greene & Sandell

Bette Greene (then Bette Evensky) with her parents in their store in Parkin; circa 1940.

John Grisham at That Bookstore in Blytheville; 2000.

JOHN GRISHAM

is a famous writer who was born in Arkansas and grew up in Arkansas. His parents were cotton farmers near Black Oak, Arkansas, when Grisham was born. His father later took jobs in construction. These jobs caused the family to move many times, but Grisham's grandparents continued to farm, and his grandfather also owned a store in Blytheville. Grisham and his brothers and sisters often visited their grandparents in Arkansas, especially after the family settled in Mississippi. Grisham loved baseball, listening to St. Louis Cardinals games on the radio. He attended colleges that had good baseball teams so he could play the game. He eventually earned a degree in accounting. He then went to law school in Mississippi, earning a law degree. Shortly after graduation from law school, Grisham married Renee Jones in 1981. He worked as a lawyer in Mississippi and was also elected to the Mississippi House of Representatives, serving from 1984 until 1990.

While he was a state representative, Grisham attended a trial that made him start asking himself questions. He wondered how things might have turned out differently if other things had been done. The more he wondered, the more he imagined a story that he thought would make an interesting book. The book he wrote, *A Time to Kill,*

Timeline

Born: February 8, 1955

Became a lawyer: 1981

sold only a few thousand copies in southern states, but it began a very successful career. His second book, *The Firm*, was listed on the *New York Times* bestseller list. Grisham began writing one novel each year. His publisher prints millions of copies of each new book, putting them into stores all over the world. More than 60 million copies of Grisham's books have been sold. Many of them have been made into movies, including *The Firm*, *The Pelican Brief*, and *The Chamber*. Grisham's books have been described as "legal thrillers," since they generally describe crimes and the lawyers who work to punish criminals and to defend innocent people.

Grisham never forgot the time he spent in Arkansas. In 2001, he published a book called *A Painted House*

based on his experiences as a child in northeastern Arkansas. Two years later, the book inspired a movie of the same name. The movie was filmed in and around Lepanto. The house that was featured in the movie was made into a muse-um. Grish-

am has also helped to raise money to support Arkansas State University in Jonesboro. He has contributed generously to a magazine called the *Oxford American*, which began in Oxford, Mississippi, but now has its offices in Conway, Arkansas, and Little Rock, Arkansas.

Blyt
Lepar
Black

Courtesy of Mike Polston and the Encyclopedia of Arkansas History & Culture

The *"A Painted House"* Museum in Lepanto; 2009.

Photo courtesy of Johnelle Hunt

J. B. Hunt with some of his company's trucks.

JOHNNIE BRYANT HUNT was usually known by his initials, J. B. He was born on a farm in Cleburne County, Arkansas, and he grew up working on that farm. He left school after his seventh-grade year to take a job at his uncle's sawmill. He married Johnelle DeBusk when he was twenty-five years old. That year he took a job driving a truck. This job led him eventually to start J. B. Hunt Transport Services, which is now one of the largest trucking companies in the world and is based in Lowell, Arkansas.

Hunt had wanted to make money raising chickens, as Donald Tyson was already doing. Driving through the Stuttgart, Arkansas, area around 1960, Hunt noticed that the rice farmers in the area were burning the hulls from their rice. (Hulls are hard shells that cover the part of the rice plant that is eaten.) Hunt knew that those hulls could be made into bedding for chickens. He visited some rice farmers and convinced them to sell him their unwanted hulls. In 1961, Hunt started a company in Stuttgart to make poultry bedding. He lost almost $20,000 his first year, but soon his company was making a profit. In 1969, his growing company bought its own trucks to transport the bedding. By 1983, the trucking part of his company was so successful that Hunt decided to sell the poultry bedding business and focus entirely on trucking.

That year, 1983, his trucking company was only the eighteenth-largest trucking business in the country. It grew quickly into one of the largest companies of its kind. One reason J. B. Hunt Transport Services grew so large is that Hunt was able to attract other large com-

Timeline

Born: February 28, 1927

Began driving a truck: 1953

"I just haul the freight and the money rolls in."

panies to use his trucks to ship their products. Sam Walton's Walmart company was one of Hunt's largest customers. In 1989, Hunt negotiated a contract with the Santa Fe Railroad to make a partnership between the two companies. Most trucking companies saw railroads as competition for their customers. Instead, Hunt found a way to combine the best aspects of railroads and large trucks. By 1993, Hunt's company was earning one billion dollars a year. By 1999, that amount had doubled. At one time, more than 16,000 people worked for Hunt's company, although the company has shrunk in recent years.

● Lowell

Stuttgart ●

J. B. Hunt was able to see an opportunity and make it work. That ability made him one of the wealthiest men in Arkansas. His ideas have changed more than one Arkansas industry. Those ideas give many people jobs. They shape the life of nearly each person who lives in Arkansas. Almost everything we buy in stores has been shipped there on trucks like those of J. B. Hunt.

Photo courtesy of Johnelle Hunt

J. B. Hunt with new technology of the 1980s.

Courtesy of Johnson Publishing Company

John H. Johnson.

JOHN H. JOHNSON

was born in and grew up in Arkansas City near the Mississippi River. His father died in an accident at the sawmill where he worked when Johnson was eight. The next year, the river flooded and Johnson and his mother had to live on a levee with their neighbors. They lived there for six weeks until the flood had ended and they could return to their homes. (A levee is a strip of high ground along a river, built to prevent the river from flooding. In 1927, levees broke in many places in Arkansas, flooding much of the state. Families like the Johnsons were able to live on unbroken parts of levees during the flood.)

During those weeks, Johnson learned how to watch people. He learned how to understand what people wanted and why they wanted it. Johnson also noticed during the flood that white people and African American people could work together if they wanted to. They did not have to be separated because of the color of their skin.

Arkansas City had no high school for African Americans in the 1930s. So Johnson and his mother moved to Chicago. He finished high school and took college classes. He also worked at an insurance company, writing for their monthly newspaper. In 1941, he married Eunice Walker. After he became editor of that newspaper, Johnson decided that he wanted to create magazines for African Americans all over the United States. In 1942, he borrowed money to begin Johnson Publishing Company. His first magazine was called *Negro Digest*. He began a magazine called

Timeline

Born: January 19, 1918   Started first magazine: 1942

> *"When I go in to see people—and I sell an occasional ad now—I never say, 'Help me because I am black,' or, 'Help me because I am a minority.' I always talk about what we can do for them."*

Ebony three years later. In 1951, he began *Jet*. Today those two magazines are read by twenty million people all over the world. They cover news about people and about things that are happening. They describe those things from an African American perspective, showing positive aspects of African American life.

Many people in Arkansas read these magazines. They are inspired by Johnson, who began life in a poor family but who became one of the richest men in the United States. Johnson was determined to use his magazines to bring people together. He did not want people to continue to be separated by race. He con-

Arkansas City

vinced advertisers that they could invest money in businesses like his. He also convinced banks that they could lend money to African Americans to help them start businesses and own property. Johnson was on the board of directors of several large businesses, including Chrysler and Twentieth Century Fox, and he advised important leaders like Presidents John F. Kennedy and Richard M. Nixon.

Courtesy of the Arkansas Department of Parks and Tourism

Birthplace of John H. Johnson in Arkansas City.

Courtesy of the UAMS Library's Historical Research Center

Samuel Kountz

SAMUEL KOUNTZ

was a doctor who specialized in transplanting kidneys and other organs. To transplant an organ means to remove it from one person and implant it in another person. Everyone is born with two kidneys but needs only one kidney. It is possible to donate a kidney to a person whose kidneys no longer work properly. Such surgery used to be very difficult, though, with a high rate of failure. Kountz's discoveries have made kidney transplants easier and safer.

Kountz was born in the small town of Lexa in eastern Arkansas.

His first school was a one-room schoolhouse. He then attended a Baptist academy in Lexa before finishing high school in Dermott. Kountz applied to the college in Pine Bluff, which was then called Arkansas Agricultural, Mechanical, and Normal College. He failed the test to enter college. But the president of the school, Lawrence A. Davis, was impressed by Kountz's determination. He allowed him to enroll in spite of his low test score. Four years later, Kountz graduated with the third-best grades in his class. He continued his classes at the University of Arkansas in Fayetteville and at what is now the University of Arkansas for Medical Sciences in Little Rock. He earned his MD (Doctor of Medicine) degree on June 8, 1958. Then he married Grace Atkin the next day.

After he finished school, Kountz worked in California. He learned from famous surgeon Roy Cohn how to transplant organs. In 1961, Kountz transplanted a kidney from a person who was not an identical twin of the person receiving the kidney. This had never been done before. By 1972, Kountz had discov-

Timeline

Born: October 20, 1930

Graduated from medical school: June 8, 1958

ered the proper medicine to help a transplanted kidney remain healthy in the second person. Because of this discovery, kidney transplants are much more common than they once were. Kountz himself performed that kind of surgery about five hundred times, not only in California, but also in Egypt and in New York, where he moved in 1972. Once, in 1976, he even performed the operation on television. Because of that program, twenty thousand people offered to donate kidneys to other people who needed them.

Kountz got sick during a visit to South Africa in 1977. He died of his sickness in New York in 1981. He was only fifty-one years old. In his short life, he wrote many papers to help other doctors learn how to help sick people. He received several special awards, including being elected president of the Society of University Surgeons in 1974. Now some awards that are given to doctors are named for Samuel Kountz.

Courtesy of the UAMS Library's Historical Research Center

Samuel Kountz the day he graduated from medical school, 1958.

Blanche Lambert Lincoln.

BLANCHE LINCOLN

represented the state of Arkansas in the United States House of Representatives for four years and in the United States Senate for twelve years. She was the second woman from Arkansas to serve in the Senate and—at the time she was elected—was one of nine female senators in the hundred-member body. She was born in Helena, Arkansas, in 1960 into a farming family. Her parents, Jordan and Martha Lambert, grew rice, corn, soybeans, and cotton. The Lambert family had been farming for seven generations. Blanche Lambert went to school in Helena. She won her first election when she ran for student council president of Helena High School in 1977.

After graduating from college, Lambert moved to Washington DC.

She worked for two years as an assistant to United States Representative Bill Alexander. She then held other jobs in Washington. In 1992, Lambert moved back to Helena and began campaigning for Alexander's seat in Congress. Alexander was accused of misusing government money for his own personal use. In May, Lambert won an election over Alexander for the Democratic nomination to Congress. In November she defeated Republican candidate Terry Hayes, becoming the first woman to represent Arkansas's First Congressional District in the United States House of Representatives. The next year, she married Steve Lincoln, a doctor who lived and worked in Virginia.

In 1998, Senator Dale Bumpers announced that he would not be running to be reelected. Lincoln decided to run for the Senate. Lincoln had to win three elections to become a senator. The Democratic primary in May had four people running. Lincoln got more votes than any other candidate, but she had fewer than half the votes. Running the next month against Winston Bryant—who had come in second in May—Lincoln won again, giving her the nomination. In November, she won yet again, defeating Republican Fay Boozman by about 90,000 votes. Six years later, Lincoln was reelected to the Senate.

Timeline

Born: September 30, 1960   Worked for Congressman Bill Alexander: 1982–1984

"I am not normally a betting person, but I say that putting your money on the American people is about as close to a sure bet as you are going to get."

When she ran a third time in 2010, she lost the election to John Boozman, Fay's younger brother.

During her years in the House and the Senate, Lincoln tried to help working families, farmers, and military veterans. She served on several important committees, including the Senate Finance Committee, which makes decisions about government budgets and federal taxes. Lincoln started a new group in the United States Senate, the Hunger Caucus, to help Americans who do not have enough food. She also found ways to help the Delta Regional Authority, which helps people living in eastern Arkansas and other parts of the country near the Mississippi River.

Helena

Blanche Lincoln and her husband, Steve Lincoln, holding their sons, Reece and Bennett, while visiting President Bill Clinton.

Served in U.S. House of Representatives: 1993–1997   Served in U.S. Senate: 1999–2011

Courtesy of the University of Central Arkansas

Scottie Pippen playing basketball for the University of Central Arkansas; circa 1987.

SCOTTIE PIPPEN

is one of several famous basketball players from Arkansas. He is a hero in the city of Chicago where he played for a professional team, the Chicago Bulls. The Bulls won six championships in the 1990s. Pippen also won two gold medals playing basketball for the United States in the summer Olympics in 1992 and in 1996.

Pippen was born in Hamburg, Arkansas. He has eleven older brothers and sisters. When he was in high school, Pippen played on baseball, football, and basketball teams. Basketball was his favorite sport, but most people thought he was too small to be a successful player. After graduating from high school, he went to the University of Central Arkansas (UCA) in Conway. As a favor to his high school coach, the college coach let Pippen join the basketball team, not as a player but as the student manager of the team. Pippen still got to play basketball in college, though. He grew six inches taller and gained sixty pounds during those four years. He helped his school win championships. Because UCA was a small school, Pippen was afraid that no professional team would notice him. Several teams were interested in him, though. Pippen was the fifth person chosen by any team in 1987.

In Chicago, Pippen had a famous teammate named Michael Jordan. Some people said that Jordan and the Bulls would never win a championship. They said that Jordan was so good that the other players on the team could not contribute to winning games. Things changed after Pippen joined the Bulls. The two

Timeline

Born: September 25, 1965   Played for UCA: 1983–1987   Won championships with

of them were able to work together. They made each other better players. Because of them, the team got better. In 1996, both Jordan and Pippen were included on a list of the fifty greatest basketball players of all time. That year, the Bulls won more games than any team in their league had ever won.

Pippen has been married twice—from 1988 to 1990 to his first wife, Karen McCollum, and since 1997 to his second, Larsa Younan Pippen. Pippen retired from basketball in 2004. By then he had played for two other professional teams, but he is always remembered as one of the Bulls. He still represents the Bulls, writing articles about basketball for the Bulls team website and talking about basketball on television. He has been elected to several halls of fame including the Arkansas Sports Hall of Fame and the National Basketball Association's Naismith Memorial Basketball Hall of Fame.

Courtesy of Nathaniel S. Butler/NBAE/Getty Images

Scottie Pippen and Michael Jordan (back left) as teammates for the Chicago Bulls.

Chicago Bulls: 1991, 1992, 1993, 1996, 1997, 1998   Retired from NBA: 2004

Courtesy of the Arkansas Secretary of State's Office

Portrait of Winthrop Rockefeller as governor of Arkansas; circa 1970.

WINTHROP ROCKEFELLER, Arkansas's thirty-seventh governor, was not born in Arkansas. Rockefeller moved to Arkansas when he was forty-two years old. His family lived in New York. His grandfather, John D. Rockefeller, had founded Standard Oil. All of the Rockefellers were very wealthy. Winthrop Rockefeller's brother, Nelson, became governor of New York and ran more than once for president of the United States.

When Rockefeller came to Arkansas, he wanted to escape the busy life of New York. He purchased land on Petit Jean Mountain near Morrilton and created a model farm. He also collected automobiles. He married Barbara Sears in 1948, but they soon divorced. His second marriage, to Jeanette Edris Rockefeller, also ended in divorce in 1971.

The state's politicians noticed the wealthy new citizen and asked him to help make Arkansas more prosperous and successful. Rockefeller was appointed by Governor Orval Faubus to the Arkansas Industrial Development Commission. In nine years, partly because of Rockefeller's work on the commission, more than 600 new industrial plants opened in Arkansas, creating more than 90,000 new jobs. But Rockefeller thought he could do more good things for Arkansas if he had Faubus's job. Rockefeller ran for governor as a Republican in 1964. He lost the election to Faubus, which was not a surprise. No Republican had been elected governor in Arkansas in ninety years. Rockefeller immediately announced that he would run for governor again.

Timeline

Born: May 1, 1912

Moved to Arkansas: 1953

"It is an admission of defeat if you can't by persuasion appeal to most people."

Two years later, Rockefeller was elected governor of Arkansas. Much of his support came from the state's African American voters. Governor Faubus had tried to slow the desegregation of Arkansas's public schools. Governor Rockefeller wanted to include African Americans in the life of the state. He appointed African Americans to jobs in the state government. When civil rights leader Martin Luther King Jr. was killed, Governor Rockefeller was the only governor in a southern state to join black leaders in publicly mourning the death. As a result, Arkansas's cities did not experience the same kind of violent demonstrations that happened in many other cities at that time.

During his four years as governor, Rockefeller also tried to fix many other problems in the state. He tried to make Arkansas's prisons more fair and less cruel to the prisoners. He tried to eliminate illegal gambling in Arkansas. He tried to reorganize the government of the state so it would work more smoothly at a smaller cost. He also suggested a way of reorganizing taxes that he said would be more fair. The General Assembly did not approve of all his changes. The reorganization he had suggested did not happen until he was no longer governor. But the many changes Governor Rockefeller did accomplish made Arkansas a better state for all of its citizens.

Morrilton

Courtesy of the UALR Center for Arkansas History and Culture

Winthrop Rockefeller at the memorial service for Dr. Martin Luther King Jr., on the steps of the Arkansas State Capitol; 1968.

Governor of Arkansas: 1967–1971   Died: February 22, 1973

Courtesy of Special Collections, University of Arkansas Libraries, Fayetteville

Rodney Slater as secretary of transportation.

Slater was born in Mississippi but grew up in Marianna, Arkansas. As a child, he helped earn money for his family by picking cotton and peaches in Lee County. For most of his school years, Slater attended schools only for African Americans. Before he finished high school, though, the schools in Lee County were desegregated and Slater graduated from Lee High School. He was not allowed to play sports during his last year of school because he had been arrested for demonstrating in Marianna on Martin Luther King Jr.'s birthday. He still was offered a scholarship to Eastern Michigan University, where he became a star football player, got good grades, and earned a degree in political science and speech communications. He married attorney Cassandra Wilkins.

RODNEY SLATER

held important jobs in the government of the state of Arkansas and also in the government of the United States. As secretary of transportation, Slater was part of President Bill Clinton's cabinet from February 1997 until January 2001. Slater is a successful lawyer and businessman who helps to lead Northwest Airlines, the Smithsonian Institution, the United Way, and the Washington Nationals baseball team.

Slater then came back to Arkansas and earned a law degree from the University of Arkansas in Fayetteville. As a lawyer, he began to work for the state government. He had several significant jobs, including serving as assistant attorney

Timeline

Born: February 23, 1955   Became lawyer: 1980   Served on Arkansas Highway

> *"You know who your friends are when you're standing with them in difficult times, and they're standing with you in difficult times."*

general. Then Slater was named by Governor Bill Clinton to the Arkansas Highway Commission. After Clinton was elected president of the United States, he appointed Slater director of the Federal Highway Administration. Slater held that job for four years until he was appointed secretary of transportation.

In his various jobs, Slater worked to make transportation safer by building better roads and by helping to enact laws to protect people who are traveling. His jobs dealt with travel by air, by water, and by railroad, as well as travel in cars and trucks. He helped the United States to reach agreements with other countries about safe travel on airplanes. When he was head of the Federal Highway Administration, Slater assisted in the rebuilding of roads and bridges in California after a devastating earthquake. Slater and his family now live in Washington DC. But he frequently visits Arkansas, and he has received many awards from various groups in his home state.

Rodney Slater with Governor Bill Clinton.

Courtesy of the Arkansas Democrat-Gazette, copyright 2012

Mary Steenburgen at the Argenta Community Theater; 2011.

MARY STEENBURGEN

was born in Newport, Arkansas. When she was three years old, her family moved to North Little Rock. Her father had a job with the railroad. Steenburgen took dance lessons and also loved to read books. When she was eight, she saw *The Music Man* performed at the Robinson Center in Little Rock. She fell in love with theater. Her first chance to act came when she was in high school. She played the part of Emily in the play *Our Town*.

Steenburgen went to college for a year at Hendrix College in Conway. She took classes in drama. She then moved to New York City to look for chances to improve her acting and to find jobs as an actress. After gaining experience at a playhouse, Steenburgen began auditioning for movies. A famous actor named Jack Nicholson saw her waiting to audition for a movie he was making and gave her a script. She appeared in that movie with Nicholson and then began acting in other movies. Some of the movies in which she has appeared are *Melvin and Howard*, *Back to the Future III*, *Elf*, and *Nixon*—in which she played the president's mother. Steenburgen won an Academy Award for her acting in *Melvin and Howard*. She has also been in many television programs.

Steenburgen also appeared in a movie called *End of the Line*. That movie was very special to her both

Timeline

Born: February 8, 1953

First movie role: 1978

"Talent is important, luck is debatable, but what is important is courage."

---

because it was filmed in Arkansas and because it is about railroads. She was executive producer of the movie, which means that she helped to plan it and put it together. She also appeared in the movie. Her father played a small part in the movie, too. Steenburgen is married to actor Ted Danson. The couple owns three homes, including one in Little Rock. In addition to acting, Steenburgen loves to paint. She supports many organizations that help people, including Arkansas Children's Hospital and Heifer International.

Conway

North Little Rock

Little Rock

Courtesy of the North Little Rock School District and the Butler Center for Arkansas Studies, with the permission of Mary Steenburgen

Mary Steenburgen as a high school student playing Emily in the school play Our Town.

Won Academy Award: 1981   Produced *End of the Line*: 1987

Courtesy of Matt Bradley

Don Tyson.

Donald Tyson was born in Kansas. While he was still a baby, his family moved to Springdale in northwestern Arkansas. His father, John Tyson, started a poultry business. He bought chickens from farmers and drove the meat to large cities such as Kansas City, St. Louis, and Chicago. At that time, most chickens were raised by families living on farms. Each farm had just a few chickens. The Tyson family realized that they could make more money if they controlled every step of production: hatching the eggs, raising the chickens, processing the meat, and finally transporting the meat to stores. Don Tyson started taking college classes at the University of Arkansas in Fayetteville. But he left college to work in the family business. He took different jobs in Tyson Foods so he would know how to do all the work in the company. In 1952, he married Twilla Jean Womochil.

THE TYSON FAMILY

changed the way chickens and other farm animals are raised and sold. When Don Tyson took over Tyson Foods, Inc., after his father died in 1967, it was one of many poultry processing companies in the United States. When Tyson retired in 2001, his company was the largest of its kind in the world. Tyson had about one billion dollars when he died in 2011.

Timeline

Born: April 21, 1930   Opened first poultry processing center: 1958

"People make a business. Not numbers, not chickens, not anything else. People make a business."

Tyson's main rule for business was "grow or die." The more money his company made, the more he invested that money in improving the company even more. He also bought other meat-producing companies, including Holly Farms, one of Tyson's biggest competitors. Tyson introduced a new line of chickens for cooking called Rock Cornish hens. He also made a deal with McDonald's restaurants to sell Chicken McNuggets. Tyson Foods does not only raise and sell chicken; it is also involved in processing beef and pork. The Tyson Foods logo can be seen on many meat products in grocery stores all over the world.

Springdale
Fayetteville

Large meat-processing companies did not exist when Don Tyson was born in 1930. Now most of the meat that Americans eat comes from companies like Tyson Foods. Springdale had fewer than 3,000 people when the Tysons moved there. Now it has nearly 70,000 citizens. Tyson Foods employs 115,000 workers in more than 400 locations around the world.

Courtesy of Broiler Industry Magazine and Tyson Foods, Inc.

Don Tyson (left) with his father; circa 1959.

Became president of Tyson Foods: 1966

Died: January 6, 2011

Hazel Walker (center) and the All American Redheads.

HAZEL WALKER

was a famous basketball player from Arkansas. She owned, managed, and starred on a team called the Arkansas Travelers. Before she created that team in 1949, Walker had already won awards and championships playing basketball for other teams.

Hazel Walker was born on her parents' farm near Oak Hill, Arkansas. She went to high school in Ashdown, which is where she first played basketball. She won several awards for the Ashdown team, the Pantherettes. The team traveled to Little Rock to play in a championship game in 1932. They lost the game, but Walker was named All-State (meaning that she was one of the best players in Arkansas) and also was identified as the "Most Beautiful Girl in the Tournament." Walker then went to college in Tulsa, Oklahoma. That school had a basketball team in the Amateur Athletic Union (AAU). In 1934, the Tulsa Business College Stenographers won the national championship in the AAU. Walker was named All-American, which meant that she was one of the best female basketball players in the country.

Walker's first job out of college was bookkeeping for Lion Oil in El Dorado. She played basketball for the company team, the Oilers, until 1936. Walker married a man who worked for the railroad, Gene

Timeline

Born: August 8, 1914   Played amateur basketball: 1928–1946

"My parents thought I was crazy to work so hard at basketball."

Crutcher. In 1936, they moved to Little Rock, and she began playing basketball for the Lewis & Norwood Flyers. In her five years with the Flyers, Walker and her teammates won three national championships. Tragedy struck, though, when Walker's husband was killed in a railroad accident in 1940. Then World War II caused many changes in Arkansas and the rest of the country, and the Flyers disbanded. Walker was able to play for other amateur teams during the war. In 1946, she joined a professional team, the All American Red Heads. The team traveled around the country, competing with both men's and women's teams, and playing an entertaining style of basketball like that of the Harlem Globetrotters.

In 1949, Walker formed her own team, the Arkansas Travelers. Like the All American Red Heads, the Travelers traveled from town to town, taking on a different team each night. In a season, they would play 220 games. In sixteen seasons, the Travelers won more than four-fifths of their games. In one season, they won 201 games and lost only nineteen. In addition to starring for the team, Walker also challenged spectators to a contest shooting free throws. Walker claimed that she competed in such contests more than 3,500 times and never lost a contest. Finally, after playing basketball for thirty-seven years, Walker retired. After retiring, she continued to promote basketball, giving clinics in schools and helping with the Special Olympics.

Hazel Walker (hand on door handle) and the All American Redheads.

Played professional basketball: 1946–1965   Died: December 18, 1990

Courtesy of Walmart

Sam Walton, founder of Walmart.

SAM WALTON

was born in Oklahoma. As a boy he earned money delivering newspapers and selling magazine subscriptions. He worked in stores and then served in the United States Army during World War II. Walton married Helen Robson—daughter of a prominent local attorney, rancher, and politician—in 1943. When the war was over, Walton bought his first store in Newport, Arkansas. It was part of a chain of stores called Ben Franklin. Many people referred to it as a "five and dime" store, because the things it sold did not cost a lot of money.

Walton figured that if he charged less money, more people would buy things at his store and he would make a larger profit. He also thought he could save money by letting customers find what they wanted and bring it to a cashier at the front of the store. In most stores, people waited at the front of the store while the cashier brought them what they wanted to buy. Walton looked at what was working for other stores and businesses and borrowed their ideas for his store. He was very successful with his Ben Franklin store in Newport. But he did not own the building that held his store. The owner of the building made Walton leave so the owner's son could run the store instead.

Walton moved to Bentonville and opened another Ben Franklin five and dime store. This time he bought the building that held his store. Then he began to buy more buildings and open more stores in nearby cities and towns. When the owners of the Ben Franklin chain did not take Walton's advice about how to run a successful store, he decided to create his own chain of stores. His first Walmart store opened in Rogers in 1962. Using the same ideas that had made him successful with the Ben Franklin stores, Walton became very rich and famous. He learned how to fly an airplane so he could travel from city to city. He also flew the airplane to find good locations for new Walmart stores. In 1983, Walton's company began to use satel-

Timeline

Born: March 29, 1918   Opened first store: September 1, 1945

"Don't be blinded by our own success, our status, our house, or the number of cars we own. We've got to support each other and show concern for each other."

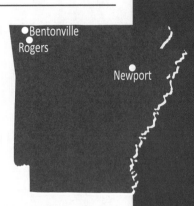

lites to keep track of delivery trucks and to know what was happening in each store. Walton built large stores that looked like warehouses. Doing this saved money. Other companies, unlike Walmart, spent a lot of money decorating their stores and keeping extra goods in another building. When Walton died in 1992, there were more than 1,700 Walmart stores in the world, and Walton left his children more than twenty billion dollars.

Walmart stores have changed the way people shop all over the world. Sam Walton's company also changed Arkansas. The Walmart headquarters in Bentonville consists of fifteen buildings and provides jobs to more than 11,000 people. More than two million people work for Walmart in more than 10,000 stores, which are in twenty-eight countries. Some people have moved to Arkansas from other countries so they can work in the Walmart headquarters. In 2011, the Walton family opened an art museum in Bentonville.

Courtesy of Walmart

Sam Walton bagging items at a Walmart store.

INDEX